FRANK LLOYD WRIGHT: SELECTED HOUSES 8 vols.
フランク・ロイド・ライトの住宅 全8巻
Edited and Photographed by Yukio Futagawa
Text by Bruce Brooks Pfeiffer
企画・撮影：二川幸夫／文：ブルース・B・ファイファー／翻訳：玉井一匡

『フランク・ロイド・ライトの住宅』シリーズは、計画案も含め640軒にも及ぶ住宅作品の中から、特に秀れた55軒を選び、プレイリー・ハウス、コンクリート・ブロックの住宅、ユーソニアン・ハウス等、各テーマのもとに分類したものである。このうち、タリアセン、タリアセン・ウェスト、落水荘は各1巻とし、これまで捉えきれなかった全貌を初めて明らかにしたものである。ライト・ファンデーションの全面的な協力によるオリジナル・ドローイングの掲載と新たに撮影した細部に至るまでの多くの写真により、真の住まいのあり方、ライトの空間の本質が明らかとなろう。

A new series of books, that deals with Wright's designs for houses, mainly a cross section of those that were built, is now published. The series is divided into eight volumes, namely by eight different categories. Three of the books are "solos": Wright's own Taliesin, in Wisconsin, and his Taliesin West, in Arizona, and Kaufmann's "Fallingwater." Another volume deals with the prairie houses from 1893 to 1916; another with the work in concrete block; work in brick; the Usonian House; and so forth. From the Frank Lloyd Wright Archives material has been selected to create a text for the books, as well as illustrate them with original drawings. These buildings are as with all of the work of Frank Lloyd Wright, so third-dimensional that they often escape the "camera's eye." But Yukio Futagawa again proves his remarkable ability to understand the work, and reveal it in a style and manner clearly his own, and still respectful to the original.

1

FRANK LLOYD WRIGHT
WILLIAM H. WINSLOW
SUSAN LAWRENCE DANA
WARD W. WILLITS
ARTHUR HEURTLEY
DARWIN D. MARTIN
FREDERICK C. ROBIE
AVERY COONLEY
F.F. TOMEK
MEYER MAY
HENRY J. ALLEN
FREDERICK C. BOGK

Prairie Houses
プレイリー・ハウス

5

PAUL R. AND JEAN HANNA   GREGOR AFFLECK
HERBERT F. JOHNSON   LOWELL WALTER
LEIGH STEVENS   HERMAN T. MOSSBERG

Masterpieces in the 1930s and 40s
1930, 40年代の名作

2
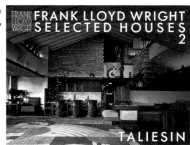

TALIESIN

Taliesin
タリアセン

6

JOHN C. PEW   GEORGE STURGES
LLOYD LEWIS   THEODORE BAIRD
STANLEY ROSENBAUM   CARLTON D. WALL
LOREN POPE   HERBERT JACOBS
GOETSCH WINCKLER   MELVYN MAXWELL SMITH
BERNARD SCHWARTZ

Usonian Houses I
ユーソニアン・ハウス I

3
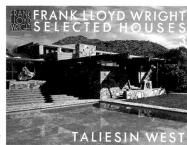

TALIESIN WEST

Taliesin West
タリアセン・ウェスト

7

CHARLES T. WELTZHEIMER   WILLIAM
SOL FRIEDMAN   ISA
WILLI   RO
ALK   ROLAND
NEILS   ROBERT LLEWELLYN WRIGHT
R ANTHONY   I.N. HAGAN

Usonian Houses II
ユーソニアン・ハウス II

4

FALLINGWATER

Fallingwater
落水荘

8
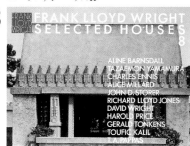

ALINE BARNSDALL
YAZAEMON YAMAMURA
CHARLES ENNIS
ALICE MILLARD
JOHN D. STORER
RICHARD LLOYD JONES
DAVID WRIGHT
HAROLD PRICE
GERALD TONKENS
TOUFIC KALIL
T.A. PAPPAS

Cast Concrete and Concrete Block Houses
コンクリート及びブロックの住宅

Size: 227×300mm/160-208 total pages (48-64 in color)/@¥4,806

FRANK LLOYD WRIGHT
フランク・ロイド・ライト全集　全12巻

企画・編集・撮影＝二川幸夫／文＝ブルース・B・ファイファー
Edited and Photographed by Yukio Futagawa　Text by Bruce Brooks Pfeiffer
翻訳＝安藤正雄，小林克弘，榎本弘之，玉井一匡

PAPERBACK
〈普及版〉発売!!

vol.1　MONOGRAPH 1887-1901　　vol.5　MONOGRAPH 1924-1936　　vol.9　PRELIMINARY STUDIES 1889-1916
vol.2　MONOGRAPH 1902-1906　　vol.6　MONOGRAPH 1937-1941　　vol.10 PRELIMINARY STUDIES 1917-1932
vol.3　MONOGRAPH 1907-1913　　vol.7　MONOGRAPH 1942-1950　　vol.11 PRELIMINARY STUDIES 1933-1959
vol.4　MONOGRAPH 1914-1923　　vol.8　MONOGRAPH 1951-1959　　vol.12 IN HIS RENDERINGS 1887-1959

サイズ300×307mm／総220-408頁（カラー24-156頁）／定価：¥8,505(1-5，9-11巻)，¥9,796(6-8巻)，¥12,000(12巻)

TADAO ANDO
DETAILS
安藤忠雄ディテール集

EDITED BY YUKIO FUTAGAWA／CRITICISM BY PETER EISENMAN

企画・編集：二川幸夫／論文：ピーター・アイゼンマン

翻訳：渡辺洋（英訳），丸山洋志（和訳）

From "Row House in Sumiyoshi" to "Church with the Light," this book contains Ando's architectural details in his unique expressions of drawings.

住吉の長屋から光の教会まで，安藤忠雄が編み出した独自の表現方法によるディテール集。

TADAO
ANDO
DETAILS

EDITED BY YUKIO FUTAGAWA
CRITICISM BY PETER EISENMAN

Size：300×307mm／168 total pages　　　　　¥4,806

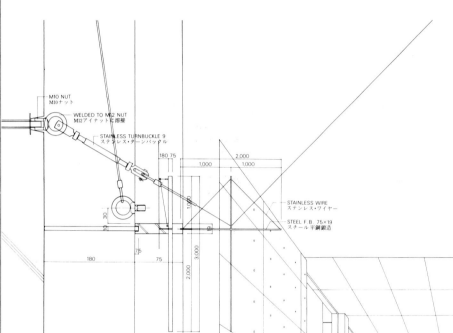

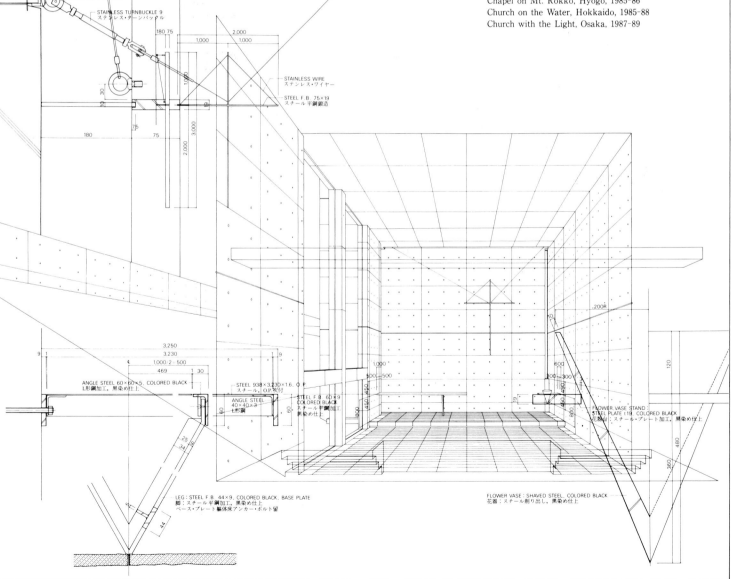

GA ARCHITECT Chronicle of Modern Architects

世界の建築家

Size: 300×307mm

表記価格には消費税は含まれておりません。

Edited and Photographed by Yukio Futagawa
Criticism by Kenneth Frampton
Project descriptions by Arata Isozaki

編集・撮影＝二川幸夫
論文＝ケネス・フランプトン
作品解説＝磯崎新
翻訳＝三宅理一，渡辺洋

VOL.1 1959-1978 (GA ARCHITECT 6)

VOL.2 1979-1986 (GA ARCHITECT 7)

ARATA ISOZAKI

磯崎新作品集

GA ARCHITECT 6
ARATA ISOZAKI 1 1959-1978

264 pages, 42 in color
Over 300 photographs
with many drawings
Size：300×307mm

総264頁／カラー42頁
サイズ：300×307mm
定価：¥6,767(特装版¥9,660)

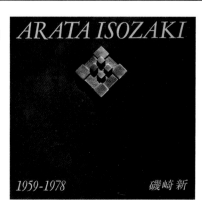

1959-1978　　磯崎新

Hard cover edition

GA ARCHITECT 7
ARATA ISOZAKI 2 1979-1986

Scheduled publishing date: May 1992
発行予定：1992年5月

1979-1986　　磯崎新

Hard cover edition

Global Architecture

GA
HOUSES

A.D.A. EDITA Tokyo

33

《世界の住宅》33
発行人：二川幸夫
編集：ウェイン藤井
編集アシスタント：小巻哲，菊池泰子
製作：谷本武彦，後藤充
営業：二川立夫，伊東克彦，引地信彦
経理：小磯義臣
写真：レトリア／二川幸夫，高瀬良夫，林正

ロゴタイプ・デザイン：細谷巖

印刷：日本写真印刷株式会社
製本：(株)丸山製本所

1992年2月10日発行
エーディーエー・エディタ・トーキョー
A. D. A. EDITA Tokyo Co., Ltd.
東京都渋谷区千駄ヶ谷 3-12-14
電話(03)3403-1581(代)　Fax(03)3497-0649

禁無断転載

ISBN4-87140-333-5 C1352

GA HOUSES 33
Publisher: *Yukio Futagawa*
Editor: *Wayne N. T. Fujii*
Associate Editors: *Satoru Komaki, Yasuko Kikuchi*
Production: *Takehiko Tanimoto, Mitsuru Gotoh*
Sales Promotion: *Tatsuo Futagawa (Overseas affairs),
Katsuhiko Itoh, Nobuhiko Hikiji*
Business Manager: *Yoshiomi Koiso*
Photography: *RETORIA: Y. Futagawa & Associated
Photographers, Yoshio Takase, Tadashi Hayashi*

Logotype Design: *Gan Hosoya*

Published in February 1992
© A. D. A. EDITA Tokyo Co., Ltd.
3-12-14 Sendagaya, Shibuya-ku, Tokyo, Japan
Tel. 03-3403-1581 Fax. 03-3497-0649
All rights reserved.

Copyright of Photographs: © *RETORIA:
Y. Futagawa & Associated Photographers*

Printed in Japan by Nissha Printing Co., Ltd.

Contents

Cover: Greenberg House by Ricardo Legorreta
pp. 6-7: Balboa Beach House by Arthur Erickson
Photos by Yukio Futagawa
pp. 8-9: House at Okayama Fukutomi by Toru Murakami
Photo by Yoshio Takase

LEGORRETA ARQUITECTOS
Greenberg House
Los Angeles, California
1988–91

Photos: Y. Futagawa

Located in a residential area of Los Angeles, this house was designed to create its own environment.

The entrance is through a courtyard limited by walls in different angles and heights. The asymmetry is emphasized by the location of a group of palm trees. The importance of the garage door is signaled by a bright yellow wall.

The back side of the house is the result of the free location of the two towers, the library and the studio, that enhance an open terrace. Below, the pool and the jacuzzi tower complete the interplay of volumes and colors.

By the use of very different types of windows, patios and colors, each room has its own atmosphere and personality. As such the everyday life offers several environments throughout the day.

Intimacy and human scale were carefully considered in the design.

ロサンジェルスの住宅街にあり，独自の住環境をつくりだすようにデザインした。

入口へは，異なった角度や高さで設置されたいくつかの壁に仕切られた中庭を経由してゆく。一群のやしの木立ちの位置が，建物の非対称性を強調し，明るい黄色の壁がガレージの扉に注意を引く。

建物の背面側では，ライブラリーと仕事場をおさめる2つのタワーの自由にとられた位置が，オープ

ンテラスを強調し，全体構成を決定している。オープンテラスの下にひろがるプールとジャクージ・タワーが，建物背面側のボリュームと色彩の相互作用を仕上げる。

多種多様な窓，パティオ，色彩を用いることによって，各部屋には，それぞれ独自の雰囲気と個性が備わった。これによって，毎日の生活は，一日を通していくつかの環境を与えられる。

暖かさと人間の尺度を保つことを注意深く配慮して設計した。

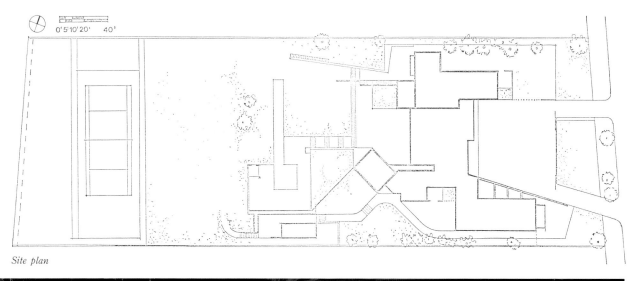

Site plan

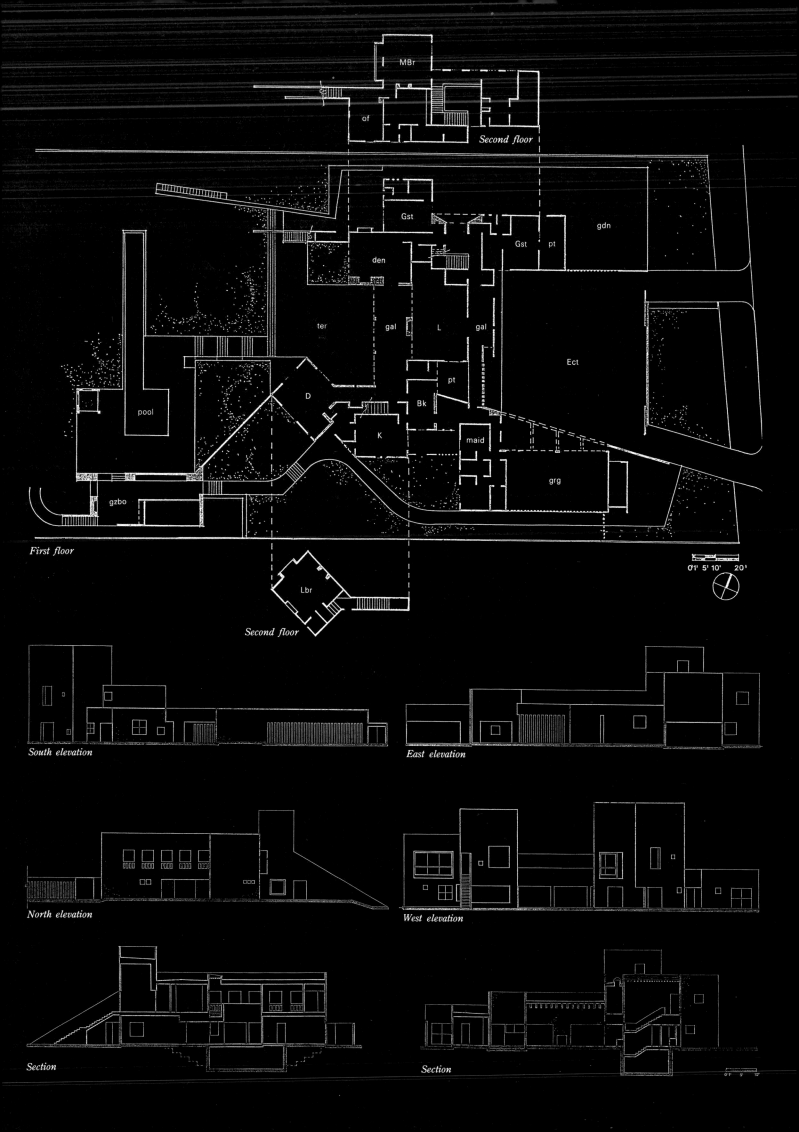

MBr

of

Second floor

Gst

den

gdn

Gst   pt

ter   gal   L   gal

Ect

D

pt

Bk

pool

K   maid

grg

gzbo

First floor

0'1' 5' 10'   20'

Lbr

Second floor

South elevation

East elevation

North elevation

West elevation

Section

Section

0' 1'   5'   10'

Architect: Legorreta Arquitectos—Ricardo
Legorreta, principal-in-charge; Noe Castro,
Gerardo Alonso, design team
Associate Architect: Sheriff and Associates
Client: Arthur & Audrey Greenberg
Consultants: Kurily Szymanski Tchirkow,
structural; G & W Consulting Electrical
Engineers, electrical; MB & A Mechanical
Engineers, mechanical; James P. Sams, Inc.,
interior; Lehrer & Sebastian, landscape
General contractor: L. B. Bovee & Sons

MACK ARCHITECTS
Summers Residence
Santa Monica, California
1989-90

Photos: Y. Futagawa

On a narrow, previously subdivided lot in Santa Monica, California, this single family house for a family of musicians was divided into two structures: a gatehouse toward the front of the property, and the principal residence toward the back.

Programmatic requirements were divided between these two structures according to their public/private nature; the main house contains all the family-oriented activities, while the gatehouse accommodates the music room, guest room, and library. Acting as a buffer between the street and the main house, the gatehouse creates a private frontyard. Within the gatehouse, an open portico was created to align with the facade of the main house. Between the two, a perforated enclosure wall for the pool was placed at an angle that provides a unique experiential perspective of the principal residence. The placement of the main house toward the back of the lot provides it with southern exposure.

Based on Adolf Loos' 'Raumplan' principles, the main house optimizes space by stacking rooms of different heights, achieving a spatial and proportional hierarchy that reflects the relative formality or informality of the rooms. Above the low entry, two floors of small rooms can be accommodated within the zoning envelope of 28′, while only the living room area has two stories of greater height. In the center of the house a basement, two floors, and a roof terrace are stacked to form the highest part of the house. The design attempts to execute a variety of spaces, outdoor rooms, terraces, and patios connected by exterior staircases. The different colors of the stuccoed facades clarify the distinct yet interrelated components of the building.

カリフォルニア州サンタモニカの，既に細分されていた狭い敷地に建つ独立住宅。音楽家一家の住むこの家は敷地前部のゲイト・ハウス，そして背部の主屋の2つの棟に分かれている。

彼らの公私両面の生活に対応して，要求されたプログラムをこの2つの棟に振り分けた。主屋は，私的な家庭生活のための場をすべて集め，ゲイト・ハウスは，音楽室，客室，書斎を収容する。この棟はまた，道路と主屋との間の緩衝地帯の役割を果たし，プライベートな前庭をつくりだす。ゲイト・ハウスには主屋のファサードと整列させて開放的なポルチコを設けた。2棟の間には，開口を穿ったプールの囲い壁を角度を振って設置し，それによって主屋を独特のパースペクティヴのもとに眺めることができるようにした。主屋を敷地の背部に配置したことにより，南に開放された構成をとることができた。

アドルフ・ロースの＜ラウム・プラン＞の原則に基づいて，主屋は，異なった天井高の部屋を積み重ねて空間を最大限に活用し，部屋の相対的な格式の差をだして，空間上，プロポーション上のヒエラルキーをつくりあげた。天井の低いエントランス・エリアの上には，小部屋のある2つの階が，ゾーニング規制である28フィートの高さ内におさまり，一方，リビング・エリア部分は2階建てなので天井は高い。住宅の中央部は，地下室，2つの階とルーフ・テラスが重なり，建物全体の中で一番高くなる部分を構成している。デザインの狙いは，変化にとんだ空間，外部階段で結ばれた戸外の部屋，テラス，パティオをつくりだすことである。仕上げのスタッコの色を変えることで，それぞれはっきり分かれているが，相互に関係をもつ建物の構成要素を明確に表現した。

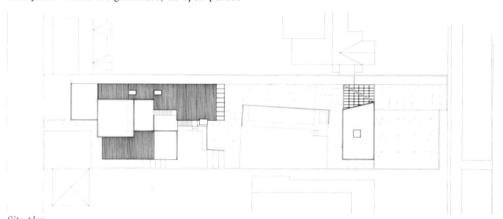

Site plan

Second floor

Br cl MBr

msic ter

Br Br

Ground floor

grg Gst/maid Lbr/D L

Eh

K F pt

Courtyard facade

Alley facade

Side elevation

Architects: Mack Architects—Mark Mack, principal; Wooi-Cheng Choong, project architect; Janet Cross, Michael Tavel, Ellen Leon, Peter Hirzel, project team
Client: Andy Summers

Consultants: Nancy Goslee Power & Associates, landscape; Martin Gantman Studio, structural; Comeau Engineers, Inc., energy; Warm Floors, mechanical
General contractor: Herman Construction

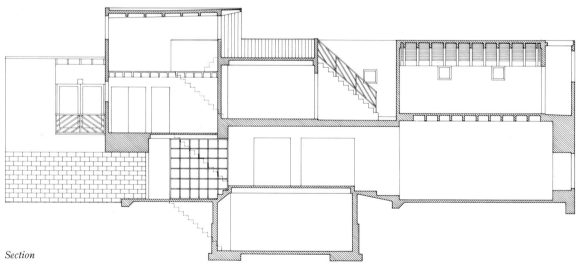

Section

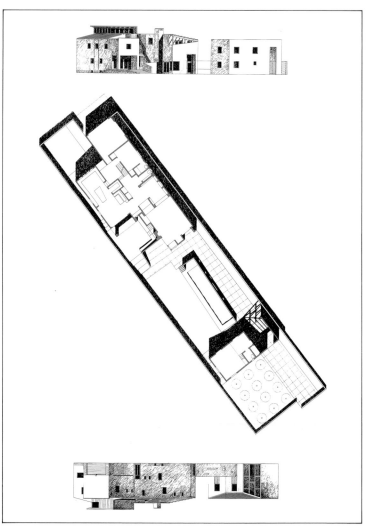

MACK ARCHITECTS
Thompson Residence
Kentfield, California
1989–90

Photos: W. Fujii

Under the shadow of the mystical Mount Tamalpais, a rather mild-mannered suburban home encompasses the ideals of a Californian suburban/rural dream: a pool, a lawn and a series of stretched-out rooms covered by a pitched roof. This alteration takes a new approach of remodelling the suburban house by inserting a significant object into the existing structure to emphasize the new condition similar to the Kelly House (*GA HOUSES* No.24). Here the addition of a trellis with an oversized living room behind and the subtraction of some of the existing program, reinforces a new order and hierarchy. This new house for a childless couple takes the provided spaces and redistributes the program in a new form to establish a direct outdoor relationship through an outdoor room and thus transforming the typical dimensions of the familiar into an eccentric and less benign image of a new lifestyle. The hierarchy of public and private spaces are reinforced through materials, i.e. a stucco front and open wood trellis at the rear of the house.

神秘的なタマルパイアス山の影の下，カリフォルニアの郊外／田園の夢の理想——プール，芝生，勾配屋根のかかる部屋の連なりが長く延びてゆく——を封じこめた，かなり穏やかな物腰の郊外住宅。この改造では，ケリー邸(GA HOUSES #24)と同じように，新しい状況を強調するために既存の建物の中に目立つオブジェをさしはさむという，郊外住宅改造のための新しい方法を用いている。ここではその背後に特大の居間のついた格子を加算し，既存のプログラムのいくつかを引き算して新しい秩序とヒエラルキーを強調した。子供のいない夫妻のためのこの新しい住宅は，戸外の部屋によって，外部との直接の関係を確立するように，新しい形態の中に，空間を再配分する。これによって，おなじみの典型的な寸法を風変わりな，そして新しいライフスタイルのもつ，おとなしいとはいえぬイメージへと変貌させる。パブリックとプライベート空間のヒエラルキーは，ここでもまた材料——すなわち，前部のスタッコと建物背面のオープンな木の格子棚で強調される。

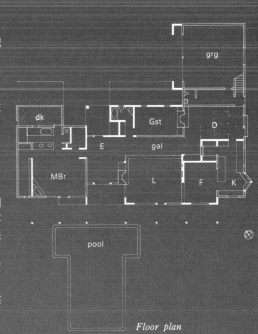

Floor plan

Architects: Mack Architects—Mark Mack,
principal; Eric Carlson, Wooi-Cheng Choong,
Chas Ehrlich, project team
Client: Karyn Planett & Geoffrey Thompson
Consultants: Rodgers Ludke, structural; Warm
Floors, mechanical; Calc-24, energy
General contractor: Floyd Construction

KAPPE ARCHITECTS/PLANNERS
Melcher Residence
Pacific Palisades, California
1986–90

Photos: Y. Futagawa

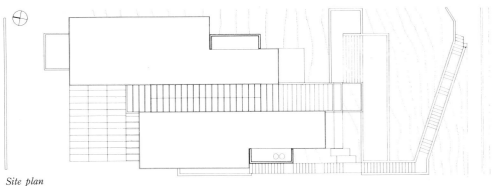

Site plan

The Melcher residence relates to the five Kappe houses presented in GA Houses 1, but it has a strong vertical emphasis. Like the Kappe residence in Pacific Palisades, it is on an uphill site, but it is on a narrower piece of property with access from both street level and from the top of the site via an access driveway. This double access determined the solution which introduces a skylit gallery/stair, bisecting the house and dividing it into several living areas.

The living room, dining room, and kitchen are to the west side of the house and are above the master bedroom. The family room, music room, guest room, and the studio loft are above the two boys' rooms. Since the house has a view to the ocean, all of the rooms were oriented to gain this view wherever possible.

The structure of the house is supported on three concrete tower units which take all of the seismic load and the vertical loads together with two front columns. Laminated beams span between these towers in a manner which has become a well-known part of Kappe's design vocabulary since the houses of the 1960's. The redwood open joist system, the teak floors and decks, the attention to detail and the fine level of finish combine to give a beautiful handicrafted quality to the house. Galvanized railings, mechanical chases, and spandrel panels are a counterpoint to the predominantly wood structure. The elegant glass floor of the galleria is a surprising use of an exciting material which transmits light to the lower level and reinforces the bisection of the elements.

The character of the house from the street below is derived from the thrusting decks and roof overhangs, but this does not prepare one for the exciting view upon entering from the carport at the top of the hill. The space doubles and triples as it cascades down the stairs and out over the living rooms towards the large outdoor decks and the view to the ocean, creating a strong anticipation to experience the house.

メルチャー邸のデザインは，「GA HOUSES #1」で紹介された5つの住宅デザインの延長上にあるが，垂直性を強調している点が異なっている。パシフィック・パリセーズのキャピー邸同様，傾斜地に建てられているが，敷地はより狭く，道路レベルからと敷地上方の車の進入路からとの二通りのアクセスがある。このことから，スカイライト付きのギャラリー／階段を導入して，家を二分し，幾つかの領域に分割するという案が決められた。

居間，食堂，台所は家の西側，主寝室の上に，家族室，音楽室，ゲストルームそしてスタジオ・ロフトは，2人の息子の部屋の上に配置した。敷地からは海が眺望でき，全ての部屋はできるだけどこからでも，海が見えるような方向に向けられている。

建物は3本のコンクリート・タワー・ユニットで支持され，これらは正面の2本の柱と共に地震荷重と垂直荷重のすべてを受け止める。集成材の梁がこれらのタワーの間に伸びているが，これは60年代に設計した数々の住宅以来，良く知られるところとなった，キャピー事務所のデザイン・ヴォキャブラリーのひとつである。アカスギのオープン・ジョイスト・システム，チーク材の床とデッキ，細部に対するこだわり，すぐれた仕上げなどが一体となり，この家に美しい手仕事の質の高さを与えている。亜鉛メッキした手摺り，金物，スパンドレル・パネルが，木が主材料となっているこの建物の対旋律をかなでている。ギャラリーの上品なガラスの床は，この魅力的な材料の意表をついた使い方であるが，ガラスは，光を下のレベルに送り，建物の二分的な性格を強調している。

敷地下の道路から見るとこの家は，突きささるようなデッキと屋根の張りだしに特徴がある。しかしこれは敷地上方のカーポートから入る際のわくわくするような場面展開を予感させるものではない。そこでは，空間は，階段を滝のように流れ落ちながら，居間の外へ，広い屋外デッキへそして海への眺望へと，二重，三重に広がってゆき，この住宅を体験することに強い期待感をいだかせる。

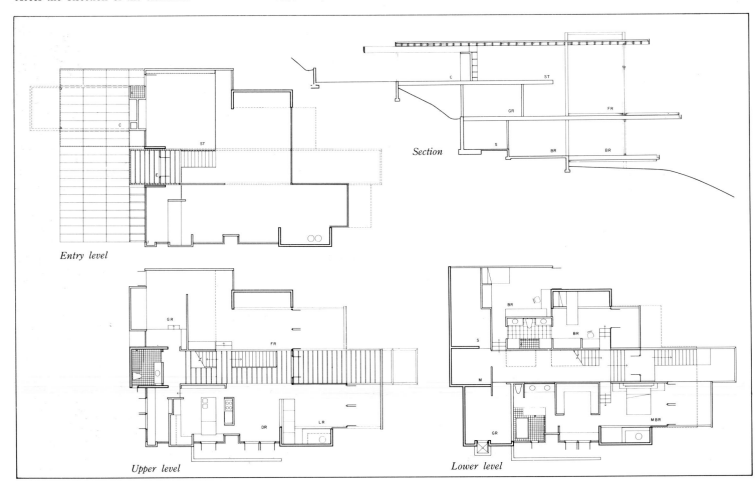

Section

Entry level

Upper level

Lower level

Section

Architects: Kappe Architects/Planners—
Raymond Kappe (principal-in-charge), Finn
Kappe, Tracy Stone, Gordon Melcher, design
team
Client: Ann & Gordon Melcher
Consultants: Reiss, Brown, Ekmeji; structural;
Anne Wait, interior
General contractor: Robert Bridges

SHOEI YOH + ARCHITECTS
A Glass House between Sea and Sky
Itoshima, Fukuoka, Japan
1984–91

Photos: Y. Futagawa

This glass house is suspended on a bluff 140 meters above sea level and faces the Sea of Japan where an extraordinary fierce wind blows in the winter. On the east side, the house overlooks a small fishing village in the distance, a golf course nearby and the whitewash spraying across the white-sand beach. In the distant north lie Islands of Tsushima and Iki-noshima, and beyond the vastness of ocean lies the round horizon. Turning west, one enjoys the most beautiful view of the sunset. On the south side, complimenting this 270° spectacle is a swimming pool sandwiched between concrete walls on east and west, beyond which the house is surrounded by grass and trees. Thus the house sits amidst 360° of natural environment that changes constantly day by day, moment by moment. The white Greek marble terrace that extends to the north, like a ship's stern, protects the house from the waves and steers a course between the sea and sky. The roof

that extends toward the south blocks the direct sunlight particular to Southern Japan in the summer, and collects the sun and serves as a poolside awning in the winter. Structurally, two concrete slabs (12m × 6m) erected vertically, suspend the horizontal slabs (12m × 18m), defining the floor and roof. The horizontal slabs are staggered toward the sea so that the house projects outward from the steep cliff, taking better advantage of the magnificent surrounding view. The simple composition of my glass house is in contrast to a glass house we have been living in for twenty years (a white 380 × 100 channel steel frame structure) which was inspired by Mies van der Rohe's Farnsworth House. A glass house set amidst nature is exposed to the unforgiving severity of the natural environment; it is also inundated with the overwhelming beauty of natural phoenomena. A glass house is by no means an ideal dwelling, there is no sense of

security or privacy and the temperature shifts are extreme. But if one could control these shortcomings, a glass house would be second to none as a dwelling in such close proximity to nature. However, this particular nature-appreciating-apparatus, swayed by the wind, floating in the air, would never be a shelter that affords comfort and security. After the drama of sunset, submerged in the majestic blue of the evening, the fishermens' lanterns start flickering on and off, this house might have been designed particularly for these moments.

Shoei Yoh

SL 140 GL ±0

SL 100

SL 50

Section

West

North

Floor plan

Site plan

71

冬は玄海颪と呼ばれる凄じい北風の吹く日本海に面した海抜140mの崖地に吊り下げられたガラスの家。東側に小さな漁村とゴルフ場，そうして白い砂浜に寄せる白波を臨み，北は遠く対島や壱岐の島を，そうして茫漠として拡がる海の向こうに丸くなった水平線を追って西に視線を移すと美しい夕景が見られる。270°の遮るもののない開放的な景観と対照的に，南側は東西のコンクリートの壁に挾まれたプールや青い芝生と木々に囲まれている。360°，見渡す限り日々刻々と変る自然景観の真只中にある。北に突き出したテラスはまるで船のへさきのように波を切り海と空を航行する。南に突き出した屋根は夏は南国の直射光を避け，冬は日溜りを作り，プールサイドのオーニングになる。形の上では，2枚のコンクリート版（12m×6m）を垂直に建てて構造体とし，その構造体から2枚の床版（12m×18m）を水平にずらして吊り下げ，床と屋根にしている。急勾配の崖地の上に跳び出させたのは，その景観のためである。この単純な構成は，20年前にミースのファンズワース邸に示唆を受けて作った私自身のガラスの家（白い，［−380×100の鉄骨造）との対比によって生まれた。自然景観の中のガラスの家は，自然環境，そうして自然現象の厳しさと同時に，美しさを過剰な迄に感知し反応する。安心感や，プライバシーもなく，

74

熱的な変化が大きく，住宅としてのガラスの家は決
して理想的ではない。しかし，それもコントロール
が可能であれば，自然にこれ程密接に肉薄すること
のできる環境は他にないだろう。これは，風に揺れ，
波に漂う自然現象鑑賞装置であって，安全で快適な
シェルターではない。落日の壮大なドラマの後，日
昏れて群青色の暗闇に溶け込んで漁火が明滅し始め
る数分間のために，このガラスの家は作られた。
　　　　　　　　　　　　　　　　　　（葉祥栄）

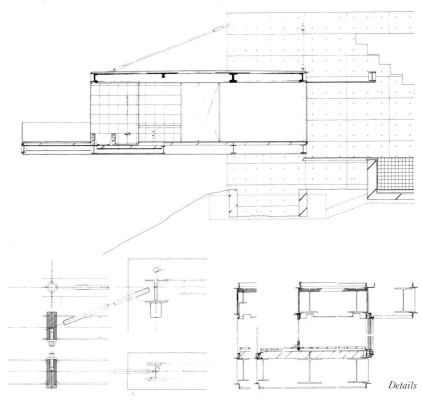

計画：空と海の間のガラスの家／福岡県糸島郡
建築設計：葉デザイン事務所
構造設計：草場建築構造計画
施工：福島工務店＋（株）エアーズ
主体構造：鉄骨鉄筋コンクリート造＋鉄骨吊構造
敷地面積：2085㎡
建築面積：216㎡
延床面積：157.5㎡

Details

ARTHUR ERICKSON
ARCHITECTS
Balboa Beach House
Newport Beach, California
1988–90

Photos: Y. Futagawa

The 4,400-square foot house takes advantage of an adjacent landscaped public way to open a 40′ × 80′ ocean front lot to views of the beach. The house, set on a poured-in-place concrete base, encloses a basement garage on the alley side and opens to the beach side on grade. A slate-covered shallow pool and waterfall separate the interior from the public beach while keeping the views open to the ocean beyond and allowing shimmering light to be reflected deep into the house. The house is approached along a limestone-clad garden wall and entered through a stainless steel gate into a patio area. The main level patios are extensions of the interior living spaces, separated only by sliding glass doors which, when fully stacked, leave corners and walls open. Floor-to-ceiling glass and glass block walls within a painted steel frame allow natural light to illuminate the house. Glass is also

used for guardrails and some interior wall finishes to help complete the feeling of a glass house. Sandblasted glass block overhanging balconies and sundeck over the entry allow diffused light below while also providing exterior areas off of the second level bedrooms. Painted steel trellises break light into small patches over the patios and bedroom walls.

The main door, in stainless steel, is entered underneath the sundeck and opens to a view of a limestone-clad steel stair. The stair is wrapped with curved glass in a sandblasted pattern and connects all three levels of the house. French limestone on floor, stairs, the living room wall, benches and pools visually unites the house with the sand of the beach. Stainless steel and white lacquer-finished wood is used for casework and doors throughout. The house's five bathrooms feature stainless steel or limestone vanities and colored spandrel glass or mirror-clad walls. Painted smooth finish gypsum board ceilings house recessed lighting, sun control blinds and audio/visual equipment.

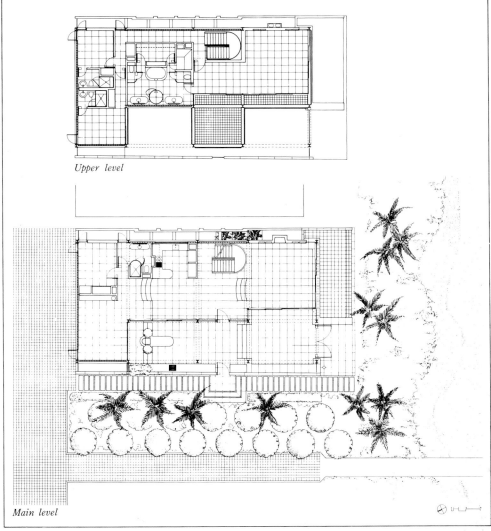

Upper level

Main level

4,400平方フィートの住宅。隣接する修景された公道のおかげで，40×80フィートの敷地からは浜辺がそのまま見える。建物は現場打ちコンクリートの土台上に据えられ，この土台は，裏路側では地下のガレージを囲み，海側にむいては地盤上に開いている。スレート貼りの浅いプールと滝を海側に設置することによって，海の眺めが見通せ，ゆらゆらと反射する光は家の奥深くまでさしこみ，その一方で室内を公共の浜辺と切り離している。石灰石貼りの庭を囲む塀に沿って進み，ステンレス・スチールの門をくぐってパティオに入る。主階のパティオはリビング・スペースの延長部であり，ガラスの引き戸だけで室内と分けられている。この戸を全部引くとコーナーを残し，壁も開く。ペイント塗りのスチール・フレームのついたガラスブロックの壁によって室内は自然光に照らされる。ガラスの家の雰囲気を完成させるために，手摺や数か所の室内の壁にもガラスが使われている。入口の上に張りだしたサンドブラスト仕上げのガラスブロック製のバルコニーとサンデッキが2階の寝室に隣接する戸外空間を提供する一方，その下の階に拡散光を落としている。

ステンレス・スチールの正面扉へはサンデッキの下を通って入る。すると石灰石被覆のスチールの階段が目に入る。階段はサンドブラストで模様のつけられた曲面ガラスで包まれ，建物の3層すべてを連絡している。床，階段，居間の壁，ベンチ，プールに用いられている石灰石が，浜辺の砂とこの家とを視覚的にむすびつける。ステンレス・スチールと白ラッカー仕上げの木材が家中の化粧仕上げの部分や扉に使われている。全部で5つの浴室はステンレス・スチールあるいは石灰石の器具に色付きスパンドレル・ガラスまたは鏡面張りの壁。なめらかなペイント仕上げの石膏ボードの天井には，埋め込み照明，太陽光制御ブラインドとオーディオ／ヴィジュアル設備が収納されている。

Architects: Arthur Erickson Architects—Arthur Erickson, principal-in-charge; Paul Murdoch, project architect; Daynard Tullis, project manager; Marcelo Igonda, project designer
Consultants: E. Brad Graves, structural; Harold T. Kushner+Associates, mechanical; G+W Consulting Engineers, electrical; Horton Lees Lighting Design, lighting; Barbara Barry, interior design
General contractor: Prelude Development Co./ Don Gittelson, project manager

ARTHUR ERICKSON
ARCHITECTS
Hugo Eppich Residence
West Vancouver, British Columbia,
Canada
1985–88 (house)/1991(furniture)

Photos: W. Fujii

Located on a south facing slope of West Vancouver, this residence was designed for the owner of a diversified manufacturing firm specializing in metal fabrication and furniture. The intent was to construct a primarily steel and glass building including custom furnishings and millwork using the materials, expertise, and labor available in the plant. The solution is a dramatic response to the challenges of a rugged, irregularly shaped site, sharply sloping to a creek bordered with abundant stands of alder, scattered evergreens and spectacular views of downtown Vancouver and the Strait of Georgia.

Linear in plan, the 6,000-square foot structure comprises three levels set perpendicularily on descending stone and concrete terraces cut parallel to the slope of the site. The main living level including swimming pool and recreation facilities separates the three childrens' level below from the parents' level above. Each of the three levels terminates in a half vault greenhouse space of glass block for privacy from neighboring residences. Glass and specially finished stainless steel wall panels are ordered by chromed stainless steel columns which support the painted white double structural steel beams.

On the east side, a water-edged terrace marks the formal entry of the house reached along a meandering pathway where the existing forest edge was carefully preserved and underplanted with indigenous rhododendrons, sword ferns and salal. The wall to the left of the entry is adorned with fragrant wisteria and clematis. The entry terrace and reflecting pool appear to be continuous with that of the mid-level on the west side, as if the building might be suspended above. The walls of these terraces are formed of fieldstone uncovered at the site during excavation and placed to the outer surface of the formwork before pouring concrete. After removal of the formwork and light sandblasting, the resulting appearance of the wall is similar to that of Wright's Taliesin, where the expression of the irregular stone dominates. Water from reflecting pools on each level cascades and disappears behind continuous planters overflowing with trailing roses along the top of each wall. The vaulted bay of the childrens' level cantilevers over the lowest pool which receives water diverted from the creek. Standing at the far west end of this pool an inverted mirror-clear reflection of the house is visible through the iris, water lillies and native river grasses creating another dimension in the landscape.

The interior, like the exterior, is a harmony of contrasts. The precise character of the building materials has created a somewhat reflective yet sometimes transparent skin in which the ever-changing natural surroundings are continually being mirrored. Similarly, inside, a palette of hard reflective materials such as chromed stainless steel, brushed aluminum and glass receive warmth from natural materials such as a blonde sandstone floor and a resawn hemlock board ceiling. Warm beige walls were choosen as a neutral background for the colorful primary accents of soft leather custom furnishings, carpets and artwork.

ウエスト・ヴァンクーヴァーの南に向いた斜面に位置し，金属製品と家具を専門分野とする多角経営を行

なっている製造会社オーナーの住宅である。この工場で提供できる材料・技術・労働力を使った特注の家具と木工製品を含め，スチールとガラスを主体とした建物を設計するのが狙いである。私たちの案は，起伏に富み，不規則な形態をもち，ハンノキの深い茂み，点在する常緑樹に縁どられ，渓流へと急傾斜し，さらにはヴァンクーヴァーのダウンタウンやジョージア海峡の壮観な眺望の効くこの敷地からの挑戦に対するドラマチックな応答である。

線形プランをもつ，6,000平方フィートの建物は，下降してゆく岩と斜面に沿って水平に設置されたコンクリート・テラスの上，テラスから直角方向に延び出る3つのレベルで構成されている。主階には，水泳プールと娯楽室があり，上階の主寝室と下階の3室から成る子供部屋とを分離させている。各レベルには，近隣の住宅からのプライバシーを守るために，ガラスブロックでできた，半円ヴォールトの温室が終端部に位置している。ガラスと特別仕上げを施したステンレス・スチール製のウォール・パネルは，白ペイント仕上げのスチール製の構造梁を支持する，クロムメッキしたステンレス・スチール製のコラムによってリズムを与えられている。

東側は，縁に水をめぐらせたテラスが，正面玄関へと続いている。ここへは，既存の森の端を注意深く保存し，原産のツツジ，タマシダ，ツツジ科の常緑の低木などの灌木をその下に植えた曲がりくねった小道を経由してくる。玄関左側の壁には，香りの高いウィスタリアやクレマチスがさらに美しさをそえている。玄関テラスとリフレクティング・プールが，西側の中間階へと続き，あたかもこの建物が上に吊り下げられているかのように見える。テラスの壁は，根切りの際に敷地から掘り起こされた自然石で形成され，コンクリートを打つ前に型枠の外側面に並べられた。型枠を外したあと，軽くサンドブラストすると，これらの壁は，不規則な石の形が特徴のある表現となっているライトのタリアセンの壁と類似したものとなった。各階にあるリフレクティング・プールから流れ出る水は，滝となり，テラスの壁の頂部にそって連続する，つるバラがあふれているプランターの裏へと消えてゆく。子供部屋のある階のヴォールト状のベイは，小川から水を引いている，一番低い位置にあるプールの上へと片持ちで突き出している。プールの西端に立つと，水面に映る反転した住宅の鏡像がアイリス，水蓮，自生の水草越しに見え，風景の中にもうひとつの位相をつくりだす。

内部は外部と同じように，対比的なものの調和である。建築材料の硬質なテクスチュアは，いくぶんか反射性をもちながら，時には透明な被膜となり，移り変わる周囲の景色を写し込みつづける。また，クロムメッキ仕上げのステンレス・スチール，磨いたアルミニウム，ガラスといった反射性の強い材料が，ブロンドの砂岩の床やベイツガ材の天井などの自然の材料で和らげられている。柔らかな革製の椅子や，カーペット，工芸品の色彩豊かなアクセントに対するニュートラルな背景として，壁には暖かなベージュ色を選択した。

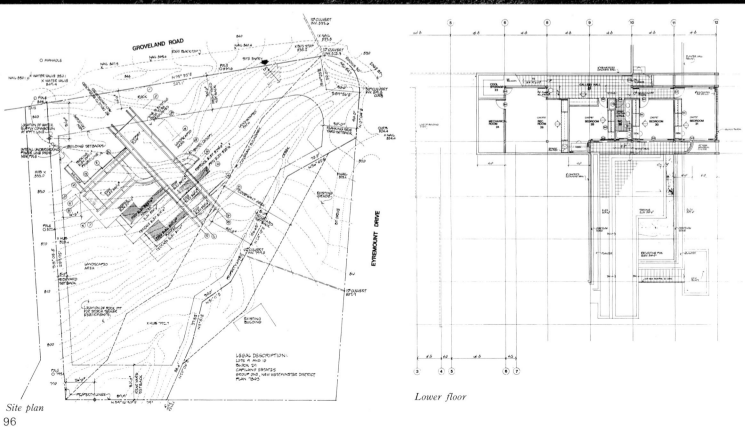

Site plan

96

Lower floor

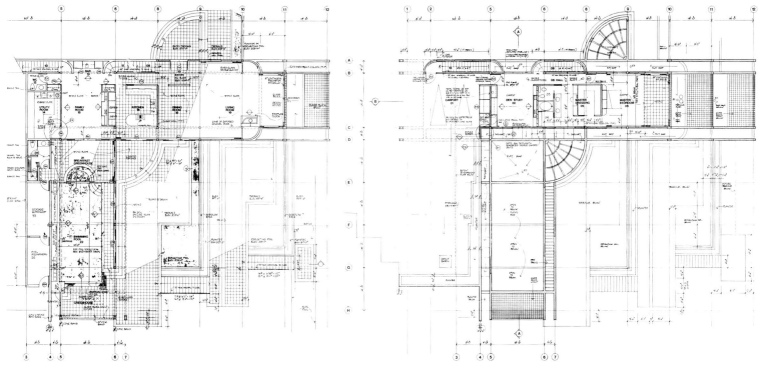

Main floor

Upper floor

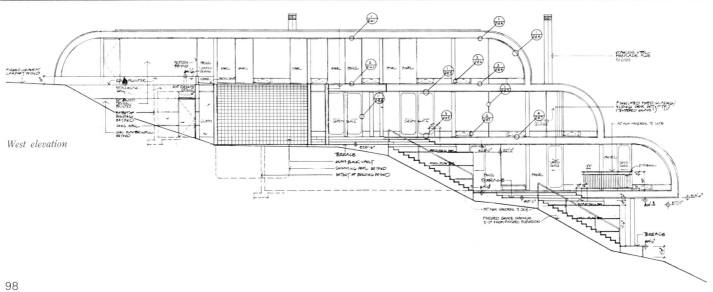

West elevation

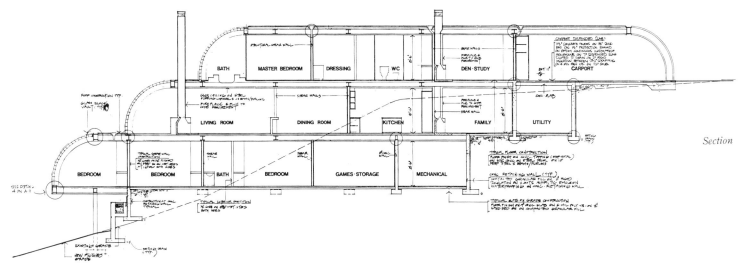

Section

Architects: Arthur Erickson Architects—Arthur Erickson, principal-in-charge; Nick Milkovich, associate-in-charge; Inara Kundzins, project architect
Client: Hugo and Brigitte Eppich
Consultants: C. Y. Loh Associates Ltd., structural; J. D. Kern & Company Ltd., mechanical; Francisco Kripacz, interior; Cornelia Hahn Oberlander, landscape
General contractor: Hugo Eppich; Stan Burton, construction supervisor

TORU MURAKAMI & ASSOCIATES
House at Okayama Fukutomi
Okayama, Okayama, Japan
1990–91

Photos: Y. Takase

The site is in a residential area that is being developed in the southern part of Okayama City. The land, reclaimed from the sea, is flat, but now the context of the residential area, including the site, has been obscured by development. The only feature to which the architect could respond was a T-intersection in front of the site. A deck was created facing the intersection, and rooms were arranged on either side. That was the extent of the architect's response to the weak place-character of the site. Roofs extend from the rooms over the deck and create an ambiguous place, half indoors and half outdoors. The result is a centripetal arrangement of rooms that seem more spacious than they are.

In the house, only the deck is open to the sky and the street. The rest looks inward. The columns and beams had to be made as small as possible in section in order to create an integrated space. The concrete beams are 180 millimeters square, and the columns, which double as drainpipes, are 140 millimeters in diameter.

A movable glass screen separates the deck from the street. The way people live in the house is communicated to some extent to passers-by through this screen. The deck is the central space for the occupants of the house and at the same time a stage, with the neighborhood as the audience, upon which the drama of everyday life is played. Today, Japanese houses are becoming very closed, and the streetscapes in residential areas are bland. The goal here is to create a house equipped with a device that enables passers-by to glimpse something of the family's life within.

Toru Murakami

敷地は岡山市南部の新興住宅地。元来が海であった
ため平担な地形であるが，宅地化が進んだ現在，敷
地を含めた住宅地の持つコンテクストは極めて不透
明性を帯びている。設計の唯一の手がかりは，敷地
正面に接したＴ字路であった。ここではＴ字路の延
長上にデッキを置き，両側に居室を配することによ
り全体を構成し，数少ない場所性を反映させている。
デッキには居室上部から屋根が披さり，半外部・半
内部とも言える曖昧な場としながら，限られた室内
に広がりを与え，求心的となるようにその形状を決
定している。
　住宅はデッキ部分のみが道と空に開かれ，その他
は内側に閉じる構成となっている。全体を一体空間
にするために柱梁断面を最小にする必要があった。
ここでのコンクリート造による繋ぎ梁は180角，竪樋
を兼ねたスチール柱は140φである。

　デッキと道はガラスの可動式スクリーンで仕切ら
れている。内での生活は，このスクリーンを通し道
を行き交う人々へと柔らかく伝達される。ここでの
デッキは住み手の生活の中心的空間であると同時に，
周囲の環境に対して生活という名の劇を語りかける
ための舞台ともなっている。住宅において生活のも
つ表情が内へ内へと閉ざされ，周囲に対して味気ない
い住宅の風景が一般的に形成されている現在，失わ
れてしまった日本の住まいにおける生活の気配や家
族の生活が見え隠れする装置的な住宅を，残された
自然的要因の中に求めている。　　　　（村上徹）

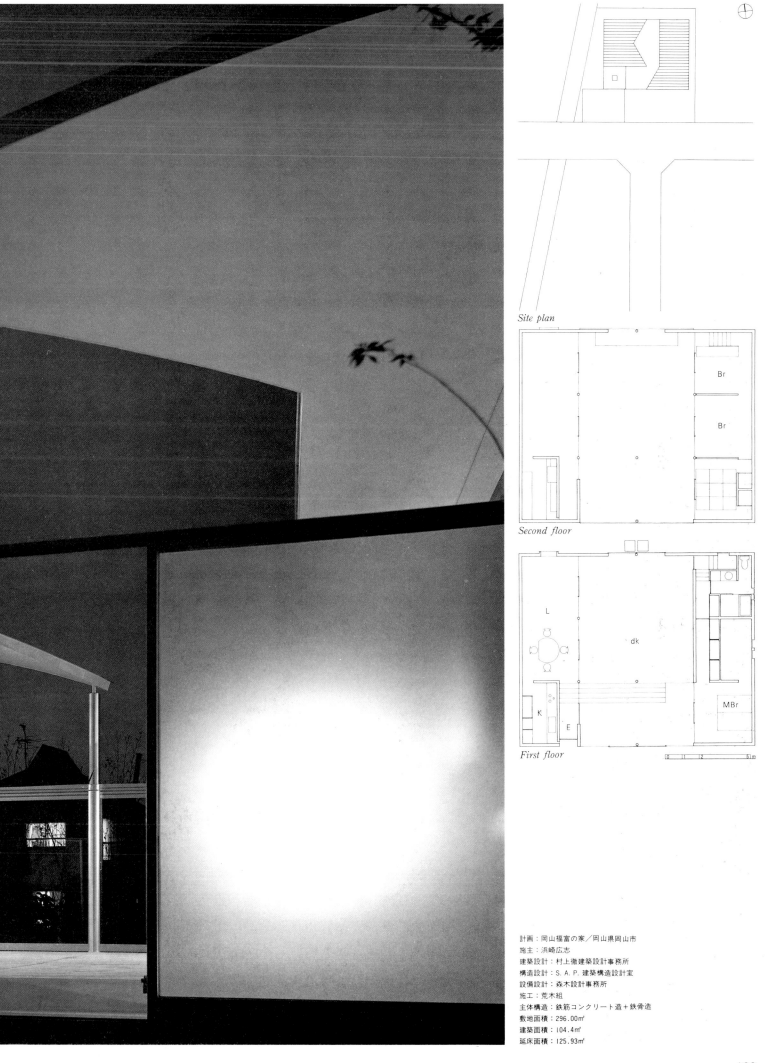

Site plan

Second floor

Br

Br

First floor

L

dk

K

E

MBr

0 1 2   5 m

計画：岡山福富の家／岡山県岡山市
施主：浜崎広志
建築設計：村上徹建築設計事務所
構造設計：S.A.P.建築構造設計室
設備設計：森木設計事務所
施工：荒木組
主体構造：鉄筋コンクリート造＋鉄骨造
敷地面積：296.00㎡
建築面積：104.4㎡
延床面積：125.93㎡

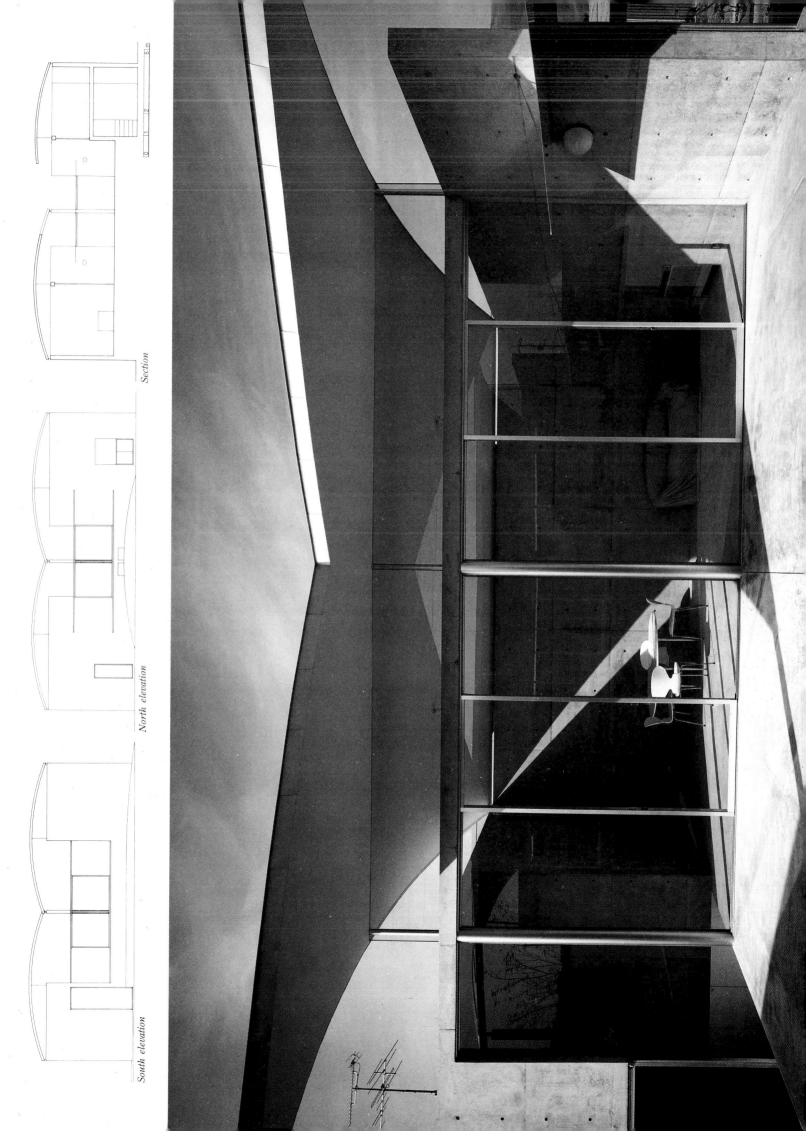

South elevation

North elevation

Section

0 1 2 5 1 m

TORU MURAKAMI & ASSOCIATES
House at Shikigaoka
Hatsukaichi, Hiroshima, Japan
1989–90

Photos: Y. Takase

The site, located in a terraced housing estate that is currently being developed, is quite distinctive. There is a park on the east side, and the view opens up considerably in that direction. Beyond the park is the Inland Sea with scattered islands, and the city can be seen at the foot of the mountain. On the other two sides of the site are streets. (The street to the north is planted with greenery.)

This project is a combination of reinforced concrete wall construction and wood frame construction. The distinctive geometry that results from the mixing of two materials and two methods of construction has been used to create a form responsive to the character of the site. The task has been to create a transparent residential space for an environment that is both closed and open. Everything is based on a planning grid 3.6 meters square. This was arrived at after taking into consideration the convertibility and the economy of the two methods of construction and the basic unit of the residential space. The wood columns and beams are 180 millimeters square in section and are the same thickness as the freestanding concrete walls. The exposed concrete and the wood are treated so that one feels them to be similar materials. In other words, the exposed concrete are made to seem lighter, and the wood is made to seem heavier. There is tension where the surfaces of the two materials meet.

The extended approach and ramp leading from the street to the entrance, the narrow passageway, and the open deck are half-outdoor spaces that link the various rooms of the house. In moving from room to room, one comes into contact with nature. The two-story volume that projects out onto an open court full of greenery is to be used by children in the future. The functions of these rooms will change—from a study and a tatami room to children's rooms—as the family grows.
Toru Murakami

Site plan

First floor

Second floor

E

MBr

str

dk

L

K

ひな段状の新興住宅団地の中ではあるが，この敷地には際立った特徴がある。東側が公園に隣接し，視界は大きく開かれている。公園の向こうに瀬戸内海とそれに点在する島々，麓には市街が遠望できる。しかも他の2面も道路(北側は緑道)に面している。

　ここでは鉄筋コンクリート造による版構造と木造によるフレーム構造を採用し，2つの素材と構法を混在させた独自の幾何学性が，敷地の持つ独自性と反応しうる形態を捜し求め，閉鎖—開放という両面性を備えた環境に対して透けた住空間の成立を主題としている。すべては3,600×3,600mmの平面グリッドによる構成である。これは，2種類の構造の変換性や経済性等と住空間の基本単位とを合致させて決定している。木材による柱梁断面は180角，コンクリ

ートによる自立壁の見付け寸法と同一である。コンクリート打放しと木を極力同質量に意識させ，その素材感を均質に表出させる。すなわちコンクリート打放しはより軽く，木材はむしろ重く扱い，その緊張の接点を求め表層を決めている。

　道路から玄関まで長く引き伸されたアプローチとスロープ，細い道路，オープンデッキ等は，ここでの諸室を半外部で連続させ，諸室相互を移動するたびに自然に触れ，しかもサーキュレーションも可能としている。緑あふれるオープンコートに突き出した2層分のボリュームは，将来は子供たちの場，ここでの個室は書斎，和室，子供室などと家族の成長に合わせて変換する。　　　　　(村上徹)

計画：四季が丘の家／広島県廿日市市
施主：河口栄二
建築設計：村上徹建築設計事務所
構造設計：S. A. P. 建築構造設計室
設備設計：森木設計事務所
施工：野村建設
主体構造：鉄筋コンクリート造＋鉄骨造＋木造
敷地面積：402.82㎡
建築面積：102.64㎡
延床面積：157.35㎡

South elevation

North elevation

West elevation

East elevation

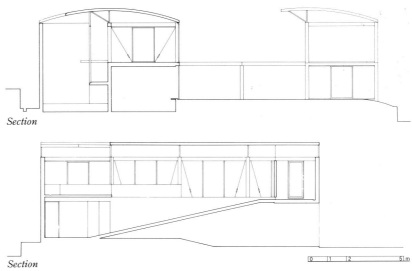

Section

Section

GWATHMEY SIEGEL &
ASSOCIATES
Steinberg Residence
East Hampton, New York
1987–89

Photos: W. Fujii

The program included a main house, pool, tennis court, and caretaker's house with guest and garage facilities on a four-acre ocean front site. The total integration of building and landscape design, each reinforcing the object/space, sequence/circulation dynamics and revelations, was primary to the overall composition.

The site sequence is asymmetrical and layered in both the north-south and east-west axis. The driveway, bound by a row of bald cyprus trees on the west and a double hedge on the east, is axial to the south and views the Atlantic Ocean through a pear tree courtyard at its end. The initial architectural revelation begins with the caretaker's structure, followed sequentially by the tennis court, "gate house"—which is a mechanical storage structure—and entry court. The main house presents a three story facade to the north, which both anchors the site, establishes a wall, and implies a gate to the dune and ocean beyond. The two story "brise-soleil" framed facade presents itself as an articulated, dynamic counterpoint.

The main entry/site stair is scaled to the garden and the ocean, defining the berm, which establishes the site level change from the lawn to the dune. The design of this residence engenders the composition with the appropriate sense of scale and anticipation. It attempts to exploit the natural site variations, both physical and perceptual, and extends the "modern vernacular" while referring to precedents embodied in the major "dune" house of the 1920's and 1930's.

大西洋に面した4エーカーの敷地。主屋，プール，テニスコート，ゲストルームおよびガレージ付きの管理人住居で構成されている。建物と景観デザインの完全な統合──物体／空間，場の継起／動線のつくりだす力学を強化し，隠れていたものを見えるようにすることが全体構成上の眼目である。

建物と景観の配置展開は，非対称で，南北及び東西軸の両方に重なってゆく。自動車の進入路は西側をサイプレスの並木，東側を二重の生け垣にはさまれ，南に軸線をむけ，その終端のセイヨウナシの植えられた中庭の先に大西洋が見える。最初に現れる建物は管理人の住居で，テニスコート，機械室のあ

る"ゲイト・ハウス"、そしてエントリーコートへと順次続いてゆく。主屋は北に3層のファサードを向け、このファサードは敷地をつなぎとめ、一枚の壁となって、砂丘とそのむこうにひろがる海への門を暗示する。2層の高さの"ブリーズ・ソレイユ"がファサードを枠取り、分節されたダイナミックな対旋律として現れる。

　主エントリー／サイトの階段は、庭と海にむけて上り、汀段を分け、芝地から砂丘へと変わる敷地レベルを確立する。この住宅のデザインは、適切なスケール感、直感力を備えた構成をつくりだし、物理的にも知覚的にも敷地の自然の多様性を生かし、20年代、30年代の大きな"砂丘"住宅の先例を参照しながら"モダン・ヴァナキュラー"の建築言語を拡大しようという試みから生まれている。

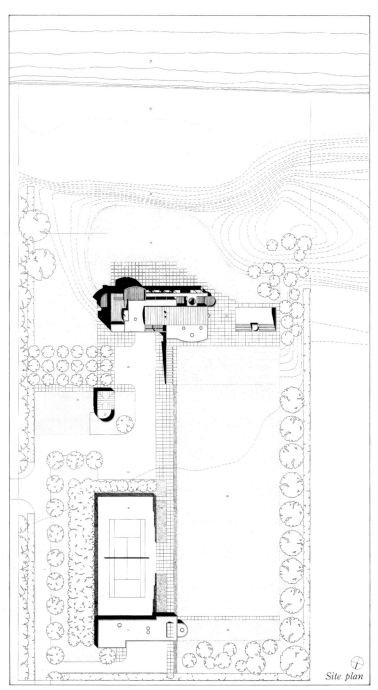

Site plan

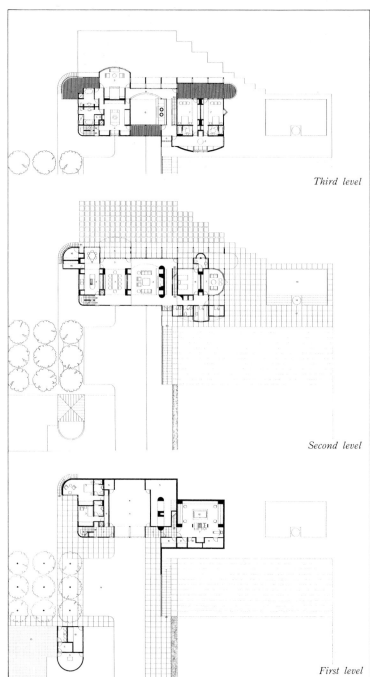

Third level

Second level

First level

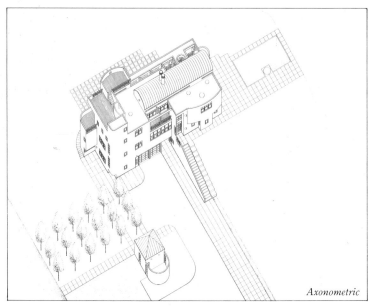

Axonometric

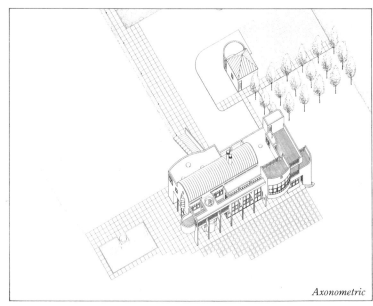

Axonometric

128

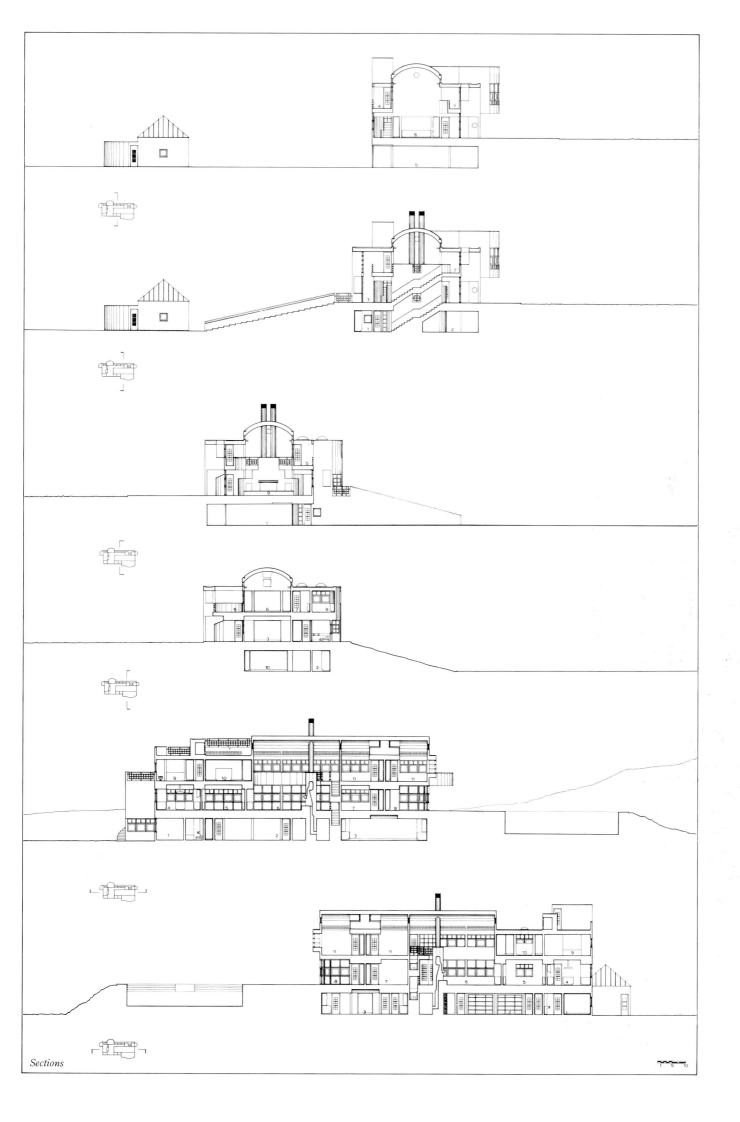

Sections

1 5 10

 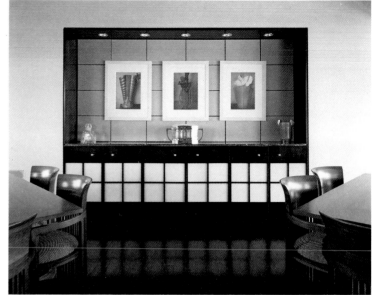

Architects: Gwathmey Siegel & Associates
Architects—Charles Gwathmey, principal-in-
charge; Gustav Rosenlof, associate-in-charge;
Joan Jasper, project architect; Joan Pierpoline,
architect

Consultants: Severud Associates, structural;
John H. Altieri, P. C., mechanical; Bachmann &
Dunn, Gale Woodworking, cabinet makers;
Linnaea Tillet, lighting
General contractor: Caramagna & Murphy

HUBERT/ZELNIO
Stewart Residence
Benedict Canyon, Los Angeles,
California
1988-90

Photos: Y. Futagawa

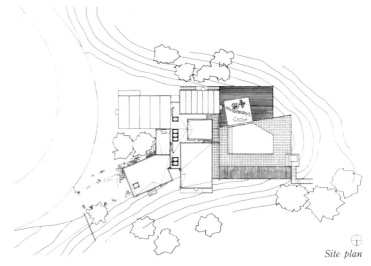

Site plan

The Stewart Residence posed a number of unusual challenges to the architects. First, the client, a general contractor, intended to build the house himself, participate actively in the design, and live with his family on the property during the course of construction. Second, when Hubert/Zelnio first became involved with the project, the site contained a segment of a house begun by the owner with a distinctive sawtooth roof, a portion of an older house slated for demolition, and a recently completed pool. The presence of these isolated and heterogeneous building fragments suggested that Hubert/Zelnio's design for the Stewart Residence evolve towards a series of discrete elements. But the constraints of the site—a narrow hilltop property in Benedict canyon and the adjacency requirements of the program tended to push the pieces back together and into a single block. The compositional strategy developed by Hubert/Zelnio reflects these competing impulses to detach and to integrate. From the street, individual parts of the house are clearly differentiated, yet the entry located between the garage structure and sawtooth piece serves as an equally evident point of connection. Perpendicular to the entry, a dramatic two story hall running north/south holds the major portions of the house together from within. Two bridges cross the hall at the upper level establishing connections between the various building elements and integrating their functions. The bridges offer dramatic views through the hall and down to the lower level, which contains the two story living room, dining room, and kitchen. Connected by secondary visual and circulation axes as well, each of these rooms provide variously framed views to the pool, deck and the canyon itself. From outside, the distinct volumes of the house are held together by a slate-clad wall. Disengaged at the north end, a free-standing segment of the wall serves as a sun screen for the large windows of the living room. To the south, the slate-cladding gives way to the copper roof which delineates the volume of the master bedroom. While the wall creates a coherent facade, the individual volumetric components of the house remain visible and establish a relationship that echoes the alternatingly integral and detached quality of the plan. This theme is further articulated by changes in and continuities of material and details which together express Hubert/Zelnio's effort to transform an assemblage of pavilions into a unified collage of space and material.

スチュワート邸は，建築家に対し，いくつもの，普通にはない挑戦を提起するものだった。第一に，建設業者であるクライアントは自ら工事を行い，設計にも積極的に参加し，工事中も家族といっしょに敷地内に住むことを考えていた。第2に，私たちがこのプロジェクトにとりかかったときには，敷地には，取り壊しが予定されていた古い住宅の一部である特徴のある鋸屋根を生かして，このクライアントがつくりはじめていた住宅の断片と，最近完成したプールが既にあった。これらの孤立した，混成的な建物の断片の存在は，私たちのデザインが，別個の部分からなる一連のエレメントを構成する方へ向かうであろうことを示唆していた。しかし，ベネディクト渓谷にある幅の狭い丘の頂上という敷地の制約と，各領域を隣接させるというプログラム上の要求は，これらの断片を集め直し，単一の棟とする方向へと押し進めるものでもあった。結局，私たちの考えた構成は，集合と離散との対立する衝動を反映させたものとなった。道路側からは，建物の個々の部分は，明白に分離して見えるが，ガレージと鋸屋根の棟のあいだに位置する入口部は，同時に，連結部として

の役割を果たしている。入口に直角にぶつかる，南北にはしる2層吹抜けたホールが，主要スペースをひとつにまとめている。ホール上方にかかる2本のブリッジが，さまざまな建物要素の間を連結し，その機能を統合している。このブリッジからは，ホールや，2層吹抜けの居間，食堂，台所のある下層の方までを広々と見渡せる。同様に，視覚上，動線上の二次的な軸線で結ばれて，これらの各部屋は，プール，デッキ，渓谷を枠どってさまざまな眺めを見せてくれる。外側からは，この住宅の個々に分かれた各ボリュームは，スレート被覆の壁で一体化されて見える。北端部では，離れて，独立して立つ壁の断片が，居間の大きな窓のためのサンスクリーンとして働いている。南に向けては，スレート被覆の壁は，銅葺屋根の主寝室のボリュームにとって代わる。このスレートの壁面が，一体化したファサードをつくりだす一方，個々のボリュームをもった各部分は認識できるように残され，交互に連結しまた離散するプランに呼応した関係をつくりだしている。それは，材料とディテールの変化と連続性によってさらに分節されると共に，パビリオンの集合体を材料と空間のコラージュへと変形させようという意図を表現している。

Architects: Hubert/Zelnio—Christian Hubert, Andie Zelnio, principals; Kerry Horne, assistant
Client: Herb Stewart and Susan Stewart
Consultant: Robert Blackwell, structural
General contractor: Herb Stewart

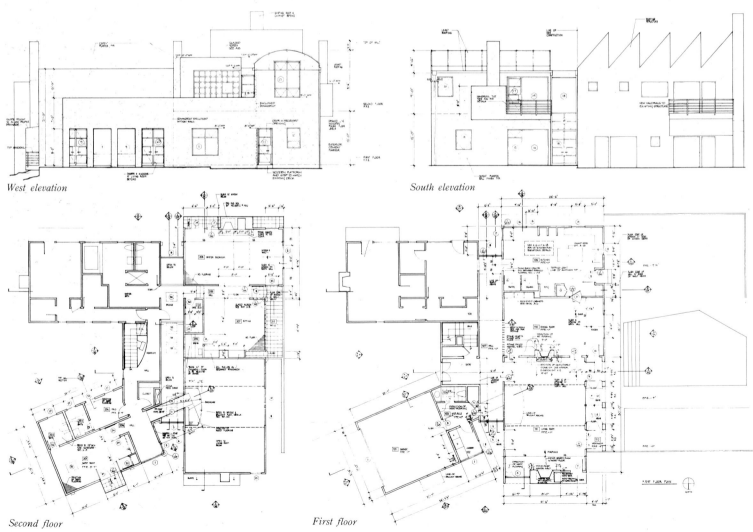

West elevation

South elevation

Second floor

First floor

KONING EIZENBERG
ARCHITECTURE
Santa Monica Residence
Santa Monica, California
1988–89

Photos: W. Fujii

This 2,700-square foot residence in Santa Monica is designed to integrate living spaces within a garden. Four discrete building elements, a garden pavilion, a barrel-vaulted house, a brick workshop with tile roof, and a lath house (carport), are juxtaposed on the site to maximize both the actual and the perceptual size of the garden and its relationship to living and working spaces.

The building elements illustrate a variety of influences expressed through differences in form, materials and scale, reinforcing the individual place in the garden and imparting a sense of accumulation over time.

Throughout the complex there is a mixing of the romantic and the modern. In the garden pavilion, a simple glazed studio rises above the rose vine covered walls of the living room. The owner plans to experiment with color on the ground floor, just as the roses will provide seasonal variations outside. The main house is a linear, semi-open plan with core elements, bathrooms and laundry, providing necessary separations. The romantic/modern attitudes are evident in the window treatments. In the second floor private areas, over-scaled double-hung windows frame views of the outdoors, while on the ground floor the large window wall with sliding sections directly expands the space out to the arbor and garden.

In the rear, the carport and workshop flank the entrance from the alley. Flowering vines covering the lathing and trees lining the alley will extend the sense of landscape beyond the gate and buildings, reinforcing the idea of buildings in a garden.

サンタモニカに建つ，2,700平方フィートの住宅。住まいの場と庭とを密接に組み合わせている。ガーデン・パビリオン，半円筒ヴォールト屋根の家，タイル屋根に煉瓦壁の仕事場，ラス仕上げの建物(駐車場)からなる4つの棟が，庭の大きさ，庭と個々の棟との関係を，実際にも，見かけの上でも最大限に生かすように，敷地に並べられている。

これらの建物は，形，材料，大きさを変えることにより，さまざまなものからの影響を受けていることを示し，庭のなかでのそれぞれの位置を強調し，長い時の流れの重なりを感じさせる。

全体に空想的なものと現代的なものとが混合している。ガーデン・パビリオンは，薔薇の蔓に覆われた居間の上に単純な形のガラス張りのスタジオがのっている。家の持ち主は，ちょうど薔薇が戸外で季節ごとに変化するように，1階の部分で色彩実験をすることを計画している。主屋は直線状のセミ・オープン・プランをもち，浴室とランドリーの入ったコアが必要な間仕切りとなっている。ロマンチックかつ現代的なあつかいは，窓の構成にはっきりと現れている。2階の私的エリアでは，大きな上げ下げ窓が戸外の景色を枠取る一方，1階の引き開けられるようになった大きな壁窓が，パビリオンと庭にむかって，空間を広げている。

建物の裏側では，カーポートと仕事場が裏通り側の入口を挟んで建っている。ラス仕上げの壁を覆う，花の咲く蔓植物と裏道を縁とる立木の列が，門や建物のむこうまで風景を広げてみせ，庭園のなかの家というデザインの意図をいっそう強めている。

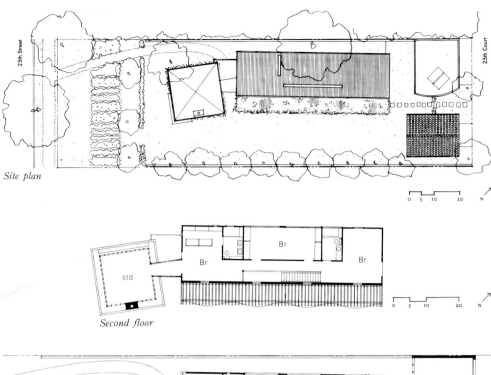

Site plan

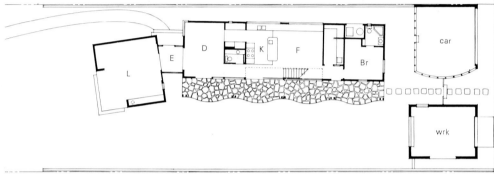

Second floor

First floor

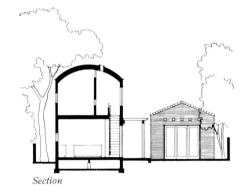

Southwest elevation   *Northeast elevation*

Section

Architects: Koning Eizenberg
Architecture—Hank Koning, Julie Eizenberg, principals-in-charge; Tim Andreas, Stuart Emmons, Yo-ichiro Hakomori, design team
Consultants: Gordon Polon, structural; Robert Fletcher, landscape
General contractor: Bruce Brown Construction

Northwest elevation

Southeast elevation

GA DOCUMENT
SPECIAL ISSUE 特別号

GA DOCUMENTの完璧な基礎資料シリーズ
A Serial Chronicle of Modern Architecture

Size: 300×297mm

1 ¥5,800
1970-1980
現代建築10年の記録

312 pages, 48 in color

2 ¥5,800
MODERN ARCHITECTURE 1851-1919
現代建築の黎明

218 pages, 24 in color

3 ¥5,806
MODERN ARCHITECTURE 1920-1945
現代建築の開花

264 pages, 23 in color

MA COMBINED ISSUE OF 2 & 3〈合本〉
MODERN ARCHITECTURE 1851-1945

466 pages, 47 in color ¥15,000

4 企画中 Planned issue
1946-1959

5 企画中 Planned issue
1960-1969

6

表記価格には消費税は含まれておりません。

GA DOCUMENT
Global Architecture

世界中で展開される現代建築の動向を探る全く新しいスタイルの建築誌。当社のモットーとする現地取材を軸として、300×297mmの大型サイズの誌面に、写真・図面・解説・論文をダイナミックに構成。

GA DOCUMENT is a totally new architectural magazine which documents the latest developments and significant works from all over the world as they happen and as realistically as possible in a generous format (300×297mm)similar to our GA series, illustrated with abundant color, black and white photographs which supplement critical essays by prominent architectural critics and historians.

Size: 300×297mm　　1～15, 18, 20, 23, 25, 29号は絶版。/ Vols.1～15, 18, 20, 23, 25, 29 are out of print.

16
〈特別号〉香港上海銀行／ノーマン・フォスター設計
〈Special Issue〉The Hongkong and Shanghai Banking Corporation by Foster Associates

144 pages, 42 in color ¥3,800

17
リポート：フランク・O・ゲリー展　評論：ジョン・パスティエ
作品：F・ゲリー、ハリウッドの図書館　計画8案他／槇文彦、京都国立近代美術館／原広司、ヤマト・インターナショナル／高松伸、織陣III／石山修武、伊豆の長八美術館／鈴木恂、マニン・ビル／安藤忠雄、OLD NEW 六甲　福原医院／他
Report: FOG Exhibition at the Walker Art Center　Essay: John Pastier
Works: F.O. Gehry *Hollywood Regional Library, Rebecca's, 8 Projects*; F. Maki *The National Museum of Modern Art, Kyoto*; H. Hara *Yamato International Bldg.*; S. Takamatsu *Origin III*; O. Ishiyama *Chohachi Art Museum*; M. Suzuki *Manin Bldg.*; T. Ando *Old New Rokko, Fukuhara Clinic, Shibuya Project*
124 pages, 52 in color ¥2,900